- help your child learn to read with expression by choosing a sentence to read aloud and demonstrating how to do this.

TIP 3 Indicators that your child is reading for meaning:
- your child will be responding to the text if he/she is self-correcting and varying his/her voice.
- your child will want to talk about what he/she is reading or is eager to turn the page to find out what will happen next.

TIP 4 Chat at the end of each chapter:
- encourage your child to recall specific details after each chapter.
- let your child pick out interesting words and discuss what they mean.
- talk about what each of you found most interesting or most important.
- ask questions about the text. These help to develop comprehension skills and awareness of the language used.

A FEW ADDITIONAL TIPS
- Read to your child regularly to demonstrate fluency, phrasing, and expression; to find out or check information; and for sharing enjoyment.
- Encourage your child to reread favorite texts to increase reading confidence and fluency.
- Check that your child is reading a range of different types of material, such as poems, jokes, and following instructions.

Series consultant, **Dr. Linda Gambrell**, Distinguished Professor of Education at Clemson University, has served as President of the National Reading Conference, the College Reading Association, and the International Reading Association.

Managing Editor Laura Gilbert
Design Manager Maxine Pedliham
Publishing Manager Julie Ferris
Art Director Ron Stobbart
Publishing Director Simon Beecroft
Pre-Production Producer Marc Staples
Senior Producer Shabana Shakir
Jacket Designers Satvir Sihota,
David McDonald

Designed and edited by Tall Tree Ltd
Designers Richard Horsford and
Malcolm Parchment
Editor Catherine Saunders

Reading Consultant
Linda B. Gambrell, Ph.D.

For Lucasfilm
Executive Editor J. W. Rinzler
Art Director Troy Alders
Keeper of the Holocron Leland Chee
Director of Publishing Carol Roeder

First American Edition, 2013
Published in the United States by DK Publishing
1450 Broadway, Suite 801, New York, NY 10018
DK, a Division of Penguin Random House LLC

Page design copyright © 2020 Dorling Kindersley Limited

22 9
017–187441–April/13

© & ™ 2020 Lucasfilm Ltd.

DK books are available at special discounts when purchased in
bulk for sales promotions, premiums, fund-raising, or
educational use. For details, contact:
DK Publishing Special Markets
1450 Broadway, Suite 801, New York, NY 10018
SpecialSales@dk.com

A catalog record for this book is available
from the Library of Congress.

ISBN: 978-1-4654-0184-7 (paperback)
ISBN: 978-1-4654-0185-4 (hardback)

Printed and bound in China

For the curious

www.dk.com

www.starwars.com

Contents

4 The greatest Jedi

6 Respected Jedi

8 Force powers

10 Size matters not

12 Wise teacher

14 Preparing future Jedi

16 Strong opinions

18 Wise Yoda

20 Yoda to the rescue

22 Epic duel

24 High General Yoda

26 Elected leader

28 Turning point

30 Order 66

32 Jedi vs. Sith

34 Yoda's sadness

36 Protecting the future

38 Into exile

40 A new pupil

42 Jedi in training

44 Not the end

46 Yoda's legacy

48 Glossary

STAR WARS™

THE LEGENDARY YODA

Written by
Catherine Saunders

The greatest Jedi

This is Yoda, defender of the galaxy, Master of the Force, and the greatest Jedi who has ever lived. How exactly did he become such a legendary Jedi?

Yoda is nearly 900 years old, but very little is known about his early life. He is from a remote planet, but which one is a mystery. Amazingly, Yoda did not know that he had Force powers until he was an adult. His path toward the Jedi began when he left his home to find work.

Galactic heroes
The Jedi believe in peace and justice. They use the light side of the Force. Their enemies are the Sith.

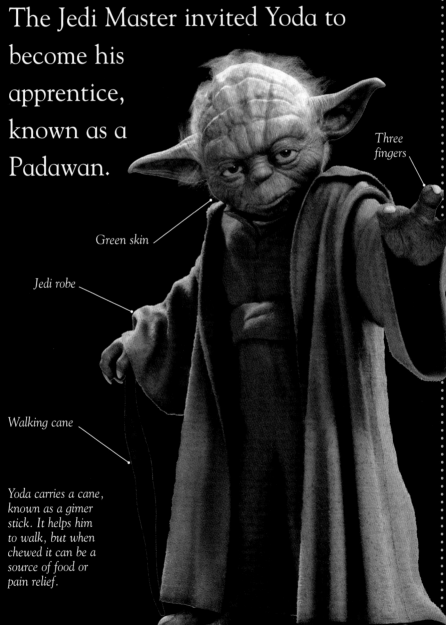

Yoda's ship crashed on a strange planet, and there he met a mysterious Jedi Master who sensed his potential. The Jedi Master invited Yoda to become his apprentice, known as a Padawan.

Three fingers

Green skin

Jedi robe

Walking cane

Yoda carries a cane, known as a gimer stick. It helps him to walk, but when chewed it can be a source of food or pain relief.

Respected Jedi

As time passed, Yoda proved himself to be a skilled Jedi. When he had completed his Padawan training, he became a Jedi Knight, which meant he could go on important missions. By the age of 96 he had become a Jedi Master. Later, Yoda was elected to join the Jedi High Council.

Finally, Yoda
became the
Grand Master,
or leader, of the
whole Jedi Order.

Jedi Master Mace Windu is head of the Jedi High Council.

Grand Master Yoda is respected
throughout the galaxy. He is famous
for his wisdom and his knowledge
of the Force.

The Jedi High Council is a group of 12 wise Jedi who guide the Order and advise the leaders of the galaxy.

Force powers

Every Jedi is trained in the ways
of the Force, the invisible energy
that surrounds all living things.
This powerful energy has a light side,
which can be used for good, and a
dark side, which can be used for evil.
Yoda's ability to use the Force is
greater than that of any other Jedi.

*Yoda can use the Force to
deflect the Sith's deadliest
weapon—Force lightning.*

Yoda has spent
many years studying
the Force and wields
its powers wisely. He
uses it to guide his

Yoda meditates using the Force.

actions and decisions, yet, if necessary,
he can also harness the power of the
Force. Yoda can use the Force to leap
great distances, lift heavy objects, and
control the minds of others.

Yoda can use the Force to lift huge rocks.
He uses the Force to throw them, too.

Size matters not

Yoda is only 66 cm (2 feet 2 inches) tall, but he is a fierce fighter. The Jedi's preferred weapon is a lightsaber and Yoda is a famous swordmaster.

There are seven main forms of lightsaber combat. Yoda's favorite style is Form IV, known as Ataru.

Lightsaber

Determined expression

Tiny feet

Yoda needs all his lightsaber skills when he duels Darth Sidious.
He has met his match in the powerful Sith Lord.

What Yoda lacks in size he makes up for in athletic ability. He uses quick jumps, twists, and turns to confuse his opponents, and draws strength from the light side of the Force. Like all Jedi, however, Yoda enters into battle only when there is no other option.

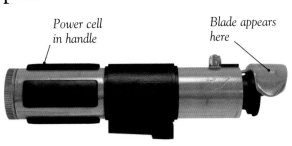

Power cell in handle

Blade appears here

Every Jedi builds his own lightsaber. Yoda's fits into his small hands perfectly.

Wise teacher

Over the years, many Jedi have been trained by the legendary Master Yoda, including Count Dooku and Ki-Adi-Mundi. No one knows more about being a Jedi, but Yoda is a tough teacher. He expects his pupils to work very hard.

Most Jedi Masters train only one Padawan apprentice at a time, but Yoda has many Jedi pupils.

Ornate cloak

Red Sith lightsaber

Count Dooku was a difficult student. He had lots of unconventional ideas about being a Jedi.

Yoda taught Count
Dooku and Ki-Adi-
Mundi how to fight with
lightsabers and how to
uphold peace and justice
in the galaxy. He also
instructed them in
the ways of the light
side of the Force.

Both Dooku and
Ki-Adi-Mundi became
skilled Jedi Knights,
and later Masters.
However, Dooku was
not happy with life as a
Jedi and left the Order.
Count Dooku's current
whereabouts and
occupation are unknown.

Lightsaber

Boots

*Ki-Adi-Mundi was
a dedicated pupil and
he is now a brave
Jedi Master.*

Preparing future Jedi

One of Yoda's most important jobs is selecting the new recruits to the Jedi Order. These recruits are known as younglings. They are sensitive to the Force, but don't know how to use their powers yet. Yoda decides who has the potential to become a Jedi.

Yoda enjoys passing on his years of knowledge to the younglings. He is a wise and patient teacher. He is also very funny! The younglings enjoy being taught by the legendary Jedi.

The younglings live and train in the Jedi Temple on Coruscant.

Jedi Master Qui-Gon Jinn believes that young Anakin Skywalker is the Chosen One—a great Jedi who will bring balance to the Force.

Strong opinions

Yoda's great age and his knowledge of the Force give him great insight into the thoughts and feelings of others. He uses his wisdom and experience to guide the Jedi Council when they are faced with difficult decisions.

Jedi Qui-Gon Jinn wants Anakin Skywalker to become a Jedi, too, but Yoda does not think it is a good idea. The boy has strong Force powers, but Anakin is too old to begin training. Yoda also senses much fear in him and advises the Jedi Council to refuse Qui-Gon's request.

Soon after, Qui-Gon is destroyed by the Sith Darth Maul. His dying wish is for Obi-Wan to train Anakin, so Yoda changes his mind.

Anakin Skywalker
Most Jedi begin their training when they are infants, but Anakin is 10 years old when he becomes a Padawan. He will become a famous Jedi Knight.

Wise Yoda

Master Yoda is famous for his wisdom. Many important people visit him if they need advice or are looking for information. When Obi-Wan Kenobi needs to locate a planet that has mysteriously disappeared from the Jedi Archives, he turns to Yoda. Sure enough, Yoda finds the answer.

Yoda tells Obi-Wan that a Jedi must have erased the planet from the Jedi Archives, but who it was or why they did it is a mystery.

Anakin dreams that his pregnant wife, Padmé, will die in childbirth. He will do anything to make sure that doesn't happen.

Anakin Skywalker has nightmares that his wife, Padmé, will die, so he asks Master Yoda for advice. Yoda warns the Jedi that fear of loss will lead him to the dark side. Sadly, Anakin doesn't listen to Yoda.

Kamino

Obi-Wan is searching for the planet Kamino. When he locates it, he finds a huge clone army there.

The Jedi go to Geonosis to rescue Padmé, Anakin, and Obi-Wan.

Yoda to the rescue

The Jedi believe in peace, freedom, and diplomacy, but sometimes conflict is the only option. Trouble has been growing in the galaxy for some time, because a group known as the Separatists want to break away from the democratic rule of the Republic.

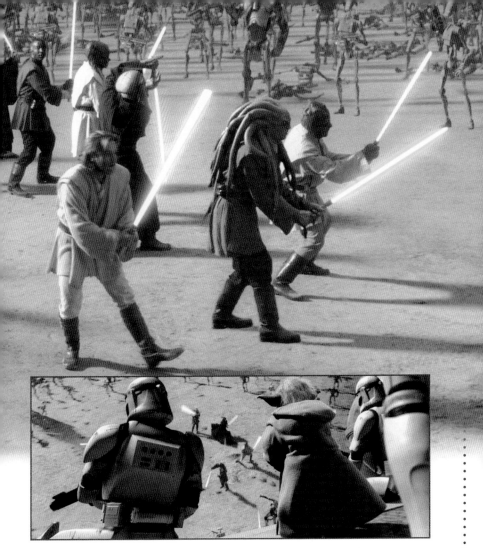

Yoda arrives with soldiers from the Clone Army Obi-Wan discovered on Kamino.

On Geonosis, the Jedi find themselves surrounded by the Separatists' huge Droid Army. Things look serious—until Master Yoda arrives with reinforcements.

Epic duel

On Geonosis, Yoda meets an old friend—Count Dooku. However, Dooku is now a Separatist leader, and therefore an enemy of the Jedi.

Anakin Skywalker and Obi-Wan Kenobi duel Dooku, but he is too powerful. It is up to Yoda to defeat him. As the Jedi and his former Padawan duel, Dooku uses Force lightning. Yoda knows that only a Sith would do that. He realizes that Dooku has turned to the dark side.

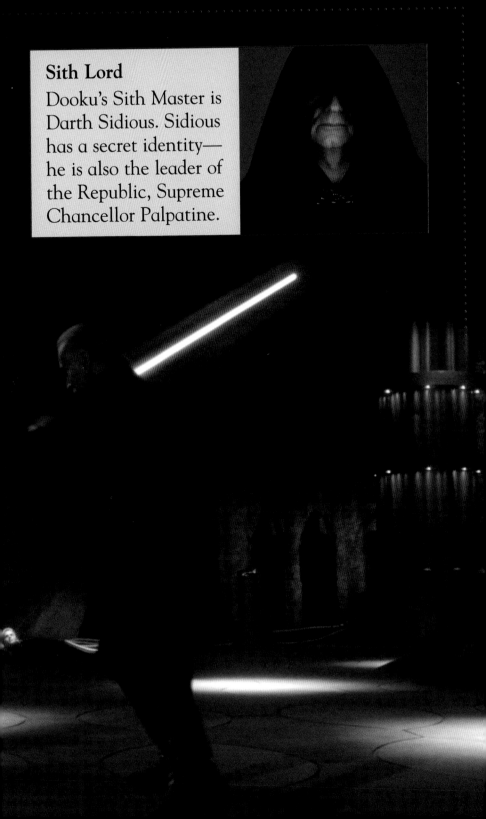

Sith Lord

Dooku's Sith Master is Darth Sidious. Sidious has a secret identity— he is also the leader of the Republic, Supreme Chancellor Palpatine.

High General Yoda

The events on Geonosis are the start of an epic galactic conflict called the Clone Wars. The Clone Army becomes the Grand Army of the Republic and fights the Separatist Droid Army in many battles.

The Clone Army is led by High General Yoda. The other Jedi also become generals and bravely fight to save the galaxy from the Separatists.

During the Clone Wars, Yoda's reputation as a great Jedi warrior grows. At the Battle of Rugosa, he defeats a battalion of battle droids with only a few clones to help him!

Clone Army
Every clone trooper is a copy, or clone, of a bounty hunter named Jango Fett. That means they all look the same. The clones are skilled and obedient fighters.

Elected leader

Yoda is the elected leader of the Jedi Council during the Clone Wars. He is now the Grand Master and Master of the Order—the oldest, wisest, and most important Jedi. Yoda's job is to guide and protect the Republic.

Sometimes Jedi, such as Ki-Adi-Mundi, attend Jedi Council meetings via hologram.

Although Yoda undertakes some important frontline missions in the Clone Wars, he also directs many battles from the Jedi Temple in Coruscant. Yoda uses his wisdom to advise the Jedi Council and to plan the Clone Army's battle tactics. The Jedi are strong fighters, but Master Yoda wants to restore peace to the galaxy as soon as possible.

Turning point

For three years, the Clone Wars rage throughout the galaxy. Many battles are fought and many lives are lost. Master Yoda senses that a Sith Lord is secretly controlling events and he is determined to find him.

Yoda must also help his old friends, the Wookiees. Their forest planet, Kashyyyk, is about to be invaded by the Separatist Droid Army, so Yoda and the Republic forces arrive to help defend it.

Clone Commander Gree, Yoda, and Chewbacca discuss their battle plans.

Wookiee friends
Tarfful is a wise leader and Chewbacca is a brave warrior. Later, Master Yoda will need their help, too.

However, neither the Republic nor the Separatists will win the Battle of Kashyyyk. Something far worse is about to happen...

Order 66

Darth Sidious gives Order 66 via hologram.

Yoda senses that a mysterious Sith is becoming very powerful, but he does not know who it is, or what he is planning. Suddenly, the truth is revealed. The clone troopers receive secret Order 66 from Darth Sidious—it tells them to turn on their Jedi generals!

Throughout the galaxy, the Clone Army turns against its allies and many brave Jedi are slaughtered. On Kashyyyk, Master Yoda is in grave danger.

Yoda senses a major disturbance in the Force: Anakin Skywalker has given in to the dark side and become the Sith lord, Darth Vader.

Fortunately, Yoda's Force powers do not let him down. He destroys the clone troopers before they can attack him. Yoda must now think quickly to save the galaxy...

Yoda has no choice. He must attack his clone troopers, or they will attack him.

Jedi vs. Sith

Yoda returns to the Jedi Temple on Coruscant and learns the terrible truth: Chancellor Palpatine is the Sith Lord Darth Sidious. Worse still, nearly all the Jedi have been murdered, including the younglings. Yoda has no choice— he must confront Darth Sidious.

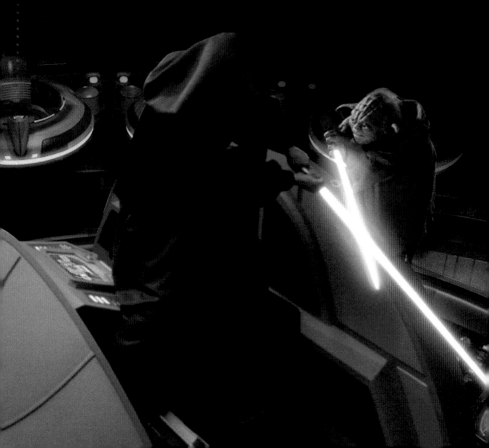

Yoda clings on to a Senatorial pod. The epic duel has drained his strength.

Sith Lord and Jedi Master are well-matched. Both are experts in lightsaber combat and Masters of the Force. Sidious is determined to prove the power of the dark side by defeating the legendary Jedi. After a duel that destroys much of the Senate, Sidious seems to have won the battle. Yoda, however, takes a secret way out. The Force has shown him what he must do, so the Jedi Master escapes.

Yoda and Darth Sidious duel inside the Galactic Senate.

Yoda's sadness

Yoda escapes from Coruscant with the help of Senator Bail Organa. They travel to Polis Massa, a remote outpost on an asteroid, where they will be safe. He has survived his duel with Darth Sidious, but Yoda is filled with sadness. Many brave Jedi have fallen, and Anakin Skywalker has turned to the dark side. Yoda deeply regrets that he did not realize Chancellor Palpatine's true identity.

Once again, Obi-Wan Kenobi needs Yoda's wisdom.

Brave Senator
Bail Organa is from the planet Alderaan. He is a loyal friend to the Jedi and a trusted Senator.

On Polis Massa, Yoda is faced with another big problem: Obi-Wan has rescued Anakin's wife, Padmé, and she is due to give birth to twins.

Protecting the future

Padmé gives birth to healthy twins, Luke and Leia, but she doesn't survive their birth. Yoda senses that the twins have strong Force powers, which means they could become great Jedi. If their Sith father finds out about them, however, he will surely want them for the dark side! So Yoda comes up with a plan to hide Luke and Leia from Darth Vader.

Yoda consults with Obi-Wan Kenobi and Bail Organa. They must find a way to keep Luke and Leia safe.

Obi-Wan gives baby Luke to his father Anakin Skywalker's stepfamily, Beru and Owen Lars.

Obi-Wan will take Luke to Tatooine, while Bail Organa will adopt Leia and raise her on Alderaan. Their father will not know of their existence. Meanwhile, Sidious is still determined to complete Order 66 and destroy the entire Jedi Order. Master Yoda must hide.

Bail Organa and his wife, Breha, have always longed for a child of their own.

Into exile

A dark time for the galaxy has begun. Most Jedi are dead or, like Yoda, in hiding. The Republic is no more and Darth Sidious has declared that he is the ruler of the Galactic Empire. As Emperor Palpatine, he will rule using fear and the power of the dark side.

Yoda chooses Dagobah as a refuge because it is remote and uninhabited. The Sith will not find him here.

Yoda builds himself a hut made of mud and parts of the ship that brought him to Dagobah.

Grand Master Yoda hides to protect himself, and also to ensure that the Jedi Order is not completely destroyed. He chooses the remote, swampy planet of Dagobah in the Outer Rim of the galaxy.

Yoda will be safe from the Sith on Dagobah. The Force has shown him that better times are to come, but it will be many years before the galaxy sees any signs of hope.

A new pupil

Yoda spends more than 20 years in exile on Dagobah. During that time, the Empire grows more powerful—and more terrible. The people of the galaxy live in growing fear.

Only a brave few dare to fight against Emperor Palpatine. These people are known as the Rebel Alliance. X-wing pilot Luke Skywalker is one of the rebels. He travels to Dagobah to find Yoda and ask him to train him to be a Jedi.

The spirit of Obi-Wan Kenobi tells Luke that he will find Yoda on Dagobah.

Future Jedi
Luke Skywalker is
the son of Anakin
Skywalker. He is a
brave rebel and has
strong Force powers.

When Luke meets a small, green
alien, however, he doesn't realize that
he is the legendary Jedi Master!
He asks him to take him to meet
Yoda. Luke has much to learn...

Jedi in training

Yoda senses that Luke Skywalker has enormous potential, but he also senses the same fear in him that led his father to the dark side. Yoda agrees to train the rebel pilot.

The training is hard. Yoda is tough on Luke because he wants to prepare him for the challenges that lie ahead. He teaches Luke how to feel and use the Force, but warns him of the power of the dark side. Luke chooses to leave Dagobah before his training is complete, but he promises to return soon.

Luke wants to save his friends from Vader, but Yoda thinks he should complete his training.

Not the end

Luke keeps his promise to Yoda and returns to Dagobah to finish his Jedi training. By this time, however, Master Yoda is sick and tells Luke that he does not have long to live.

As promised, Luke returns to Dagobah. Much has happened since he left Master Yoda. In his first duel with Darth Vader, Luke lost his right hand.

Yoda's wisdom and knowledge of the Force show him that death is simply part of nature. He does not fear it. Before he passes, Yoda tells Luke that his training is complete—he is a Jedi. But Luke's final test will be to face Darth Vader, his father, once again. As his life fades, Yoda also reveals a secret that he has kept safe for more than 20 years—there is another Skywalker. Luke has a twin sister named Leia.

Yoda's legacy

For nearly 900 years, Yoda helped to guide the Jedi Order. He went on many dangerous missions, fought bravely in many battles, and used his wisdom to help the galaxy. He was respected by those who value peace, justice, and freedom, and feared by those who use the dark side of the Force.

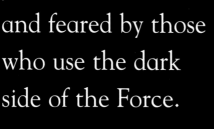

At the end of his life, Anakin Skywalker finally finds his way back to the light side of the Force.

Yoda did not live to see the Sith defeated, but for a legendary Jedi death is not the end. Yoda's Force powers are so strong that his spirit becomes one with the Force.

Like Obi-Wan Kenobi and Anakin Skywalker, Yoda will live on through the Force. As Luke Skywalker builds a new Jedi Order, Yoda will be there to guide him.

Glossary

Bounty hunter
Someone who hunts, captures, and sometimes destroys others for money.

Chancellor
The person who leads the government, known as the Senate.

Clone
An exact copy of someone or something.

Democratic
Relating to a government that is elected by the people.

Droid
A type of robot.

Duel
A battle between two people.

The Force
A mysterious energy that flows through the galaxy. It has a light side (good) and a dark side (evil).

Force lightning
Deadly rays of blue energy used by the Sith.

Galactic Empire
A group of worlds ruled over by one unelected leader, known as the Emperor.

Grand Master
The head of the Jedi Order.

Jedi
A being who has the power to use the light side of the Force.

Jedi Archives
A collection of thousands of years of knowledge, stored in the Jedi Temple.

Jedi High Council
The governing body of the Jedi Order. It is made up of 12 of the wisest Jedi and led by the Master of the Order.

Jedi Knight
A member of the Jedi Order who has studied as a Padawan under a Jedi Master, and who has passed the Jedi Trials.

Jedi Master
A rank for Jedi Knights who have performed an exceptional deed, serve on the Jedi Council, or have helped a Padawan pass the Jedi Trials.

Jedi Order
A group of beings who defend peace and justice in the galaxy.

Jedi Temple
The headquarters of the Jedi Order, located on the planet of Coruscant.

Lightsaber
A sword-like weapon with a blade made of pure energy. It is used by the Jedi and the Sith.

Master of the Order
The elected leader of the Jedi Council.

Outer Rim
The most remote part of the known galaxy.

Padawan
A youngling who is chosen to serve an apprenticeship with a Jedi Knight or Master.

Rebel Alliance
A group of rebels who want to overthrow the Empire and bring freedom back to the galaxy.

Republic
A world or group of worlds in which people vote for their leaders.

Senator
An elected representative of the government.

Separatists
Those who oppose the Galactic Republic and belong to the Confederacy of Independent Systems.

Sith
Evil beings who use the dark side of the Force.

X-wing
A rebel starfighter whose four wings are arranged in an "X" shape.

Youngling
A Force-sensitive child who is training to become a Jedi.